FIRST
WOMAN
IN CONGRESS
Jeannette Rankin

Books By Florence Meiman White

FIRST WOMAN IN CONGRESS: Jeannette Rankin
ESCAPE! The Life of Harry Houdini
LINUS PAULING: Scientist and Crusader
MALCOLM X
CESAR CHAVEZ
HOW TO LOSE YOUR BEST FRIEND
HOW TO LOSE YOUR LUNCH MONEY
YOUR FRIEND, THE TREE
YOUR FRIEND, THE INSECT
ONE BOY LIVES IN MY HOUSE
MY HOUSE IS THE NICEST PLACE

FIRST WOMAN IN CONGRESS
Jeannette Rankin

by FLORENCE MEIMAN WHITE

Illustrated with photographs

Julian Messner   New York

JULIAN MESSNER and colophon are trademarks
of Simon & Schuster, registered in the
U.S. Patent and Trademark Office.

Manufactured in the United States of America

Design by Marjorie Zaum

Library of Congress Cataloging in Publication Data

White, Florence Meiman
    First woman in Congress, Jeannette Rankin.

    Includes index.
    SUMMARY: A biography of the first woman elected to
Congress, who spent the 92 years of her life as a leader
for woman suffrage, a lobbyist, and a social reformer.
    1.   Rankin, Jeannette—Juvenile literature.   2.   Leg-
islators—United States—Biography—Juvenile literature.
3.   United States.   Congress.   House—Biography—Juvenile literature.   [1.   Rankin, Jeannette. , 2.   Feminists.
3.   Legislators]   I.   Title.
E748.R223W46   328.73'092'4 [B] [92]   80-18969
ISBN 0-671-33096-9

To the memory of my mother,
Anna Meiman,
*who was always in tune with the times
and to my daughter*
Judith,
*concerned, informed and active citizen
With love*

ACKNOWLEDGMENTS

I wish to express my gratitude to Malca Chall of the Bancroft Library of the University of California in Berkeley for guiding me to sources of information; to the good people of the Beverly Hills Public Library for their invaluable help in finding elusive facts; and to my editor, Lee Hoffman, for her open mind and willing spirit.

Contents

1
The Ranch

"JEANNETTE! JEANNETTE!" IT WAS HER FATHER'S VOICE, URGENT.

Jeannette was about to mount her mare. Instead she turned to see John Rankin hurrying toward the stables, leading his favorite horse by the reins. Why was he walking? she wondered. Was there something wrong? She ran toward him. As they drew close to each other, her eyes opened wide with horror. Blood was gushing from the horse's right side.

"What happened, Father?" Jeannette asked anxiously.

"Got caught on a barbed wire fence. Get a needle and thread, Jeannette. Quickly!"

As her father led the injured horse into the stable, Jeannette ran to the house. In a few minutes, she returned with strong thread and a darning needle, a large clean towel and a bucket of hot water.

The twelve-year-old girl got down on her knees, washed the open sore, then carefully sewed together the torn flesh. The wounded animal writhed in pain. "You'll be fine, boy," she whispered, as she laid a comforting hand on the horse's head. He turned his grateful eyes upon her.

"Good work, Jeannette. You've done a fine job." Her father's voice was filled with admiration.

John Rankin and Jeannette were not only father and daughter. They were good friends. He had great confidence in this capable daughter.

One day late in the summer, after her father had gone to the city on business, Jeannette found one of the ranch dogs moaning in agony, his foot caught in a trap. She tried to open the trap jaws. They wouldn't budge. She called one of the ranch hands for help, but he was no more successful than she. Her father would not be back until evening. Something had to be done at once.

Her lips tight with determination, Jeannette carefully amputated the foot and released the dog. When the wound healed, she made a little leather boot for the stump, like a paw, to help him get around.

When John Rankin returned to the ranch, he learned about the incident. "That eldest daughter of ours will be a remarkable woman," he said to his wife when they were alone that evening. "You're right, John," Olive Rankin agreed. "Our Jeannette can do anything she sets her mind to."

Jeannette Rankin was born on the family's ranch in western Montana on June 11, 1880, before the territory became a state. Ten years earlier, her father, John Rankin, had come to the United States from Canada in search of gold. He had not found gold, but instead he found a small pleasant village called Missoula. Although Mr. Rankin had not had much schooling, he was wise enough to see that this would be a good place to live. With new settlers migrating from the east, they would need someone to build homes for them. He was a good carpenter and soon found work.

The village grew into a town, and John Rankin prospered. He built homes, shops, a church. He saved his money, and bought a ranch in the Bitterroot Valley, six miles away in the country. With plenty of work and a ranch of his own, he began to think of a wife.

Young Olive Pickering had come from New Hampshire and was teaching in Missoula's one-room schoolhouse. John and Olive met at a barn dance one Saturday night. He asked her to dance, and she accepted. He liked this pretty and intelligent young woman. She liked this lively and ambitious young man. In a short time, they were married and went to live on the ranch. Here Jeannette, their first child, was born. As the years passed, more children were born to the Rankins. After Jeannette came Philena and Harriet, then Wellington, the only son, and three more daughters, Mary, Grace and

Edna. Philena died in childhood.

When Jeannette was five and ready for school, the family moved to Missoula. But in the summers they always returned to the ranch. The children picked berries, shared them with the animals that roamed the woods, and rode their horses around the large ranch.

Jeannette liked to gallop alongside her father as he worked with the ranch hands. She went with him on trips to his lumber camps, and often helped to cook for the crews of lumberjacks who cut down the huge trees.

The Rankins were a friendly, hospitable family. Relatives and friends, traveling in buggies and surreys, often came to Saturday night dances in the barn and Sunday afternoon dinners in the large dining room of the ranch house.

After dinner, the children would sit on the parlor rug and listen to the adults talk about the events taking place in Montana and the rest of the country. Most exciting were stories about the Indians.

There were frequent battles between the settlers and some of the seven major tribes of Indians living in Montana at that time. One of these—the Nez Perce—were being pushed off their land. There was one story that Jeannette loved—a special story of the Nez Perce Indians and their wise Chief Joseph.

Chief Joseph and his people were originally from Oregon. But in 1877, the federal government ordered them on to a reservation in Idaho. They refused to go. Rather than surrender, they chose to go to Canada, and they had to cross Montana to get there. When they reached Montana Territory, soldiers guarding the passes would not let them enter. "Give up your guns," the captain ordered. Chief Joseph refused. "We want no shooting and killing," he explained. "My people must have their guns to hunt or they will starve." The captain did not trust him and would not let the Indians through.

The soldiers devised a plan. Before dawn the next morning, they would attack the Indians, kill them and take their guns. But when the soldiers arrived at the camp of the Nez Perce, not an Indian was there. In the dead of night, Chief Joseph had led his people through the mountains to safety. Not a single soldier or enemy had been killed. Unfortunately, this was not to be the future—they would never reach Canada.

The soldiers caught up with them, and in three battles, the Indians were all either killed or captured.

Jeannette often thought of that story as she was growing up. She wondered why all people didn't settle their differences peacefully like Chief Joseph wanted to.

When the summer was over, the six Rankin children piled into a hay wagon and returned to the city and to school. Their father had built a ten-room house for his growing family. It was one of the finest in Missoula, and modern, too, with running water, a tin bathtub and central heating. Few families enjoyed such luxuries.

Jeannette loved learning new things. She had a good

memory, but sitting on a wooden bench repeating multiplication tables and spelling words over and over bored her. She liked action—to watch things being done, then do them herself, as she often did on the ranch. Restless, she gazed out of the school window and looked forward to the summer and the family's return to the ranch.

City life was not all dull. It held pleasant experiences, too. There were public celebrations with parades and brass bands. In high school, Jeannette played basketball until she broke her nose. When the river froze, the Rankin children went ice skating.

For Jeannette, the oldest, there was plenty to do at home. She learned to cook and bake and make the best lemon meringue pie the family had ever tasted. She helped her mother with the younger children during the day and read to them at night. She learned to sew, and made dresses for herself and her sisters. Nothing was too hard for her to try.

Her father now owned much property in Missoula. One night, he spoke of the trouble he was having in renting a house because there was no sidewalk in front, and he had no time to lay one. Sidewalks were made of wooden planks at that time. Jeannette laid the sidewalk and her father rented the house.

As Jeannette and her brother Wellington grew up, a special closeness developed between them. They were both concerned about people, and often sat up late talking about all the changes the United States needed to make life better for the poor.

In the 1890s men, women and children worked as much as 14 hours a day, six days a week. Factories were dirty and unhealthy places in which to work. In the copper mines of Montana, miners often lost their lives in explosions and fires because mine owners would not obey the safety laws. Children as young as six years of age worked in mines, mills and factories. They had no time to play. Tired from their hard, long work days, they often spent their half-hour lunch time sleeping on the bare floors. Many died young.

"It's unfair, Wellington! It's just not fair!" Jeannette was angry. "We must try to change things when we grow up." Her brother agreed.

In 1898, the same year that Jeannette graduated from high school, the University of Montana was established in Missoula. Few women went to college at that time. But there was no question as to what Jeannette would do. "College is the best place for a young woman with a mind like hers," Mr. and Mrs. Rankin agreed. They both wanted their children to have the finest education possible.

Jeannette was eighteen, and excited about the prospect of studying at a university. She had no idea what her life's work would be.

2
In Search of a Career

COLLEGE WAS A DISAPPOINTMENT TO JEANNETTE. THERE WERE FEW courses that satisfied her inquiring mind. There were also few professions easily available to women. They could become teachers, nurses and social workers without difficulty. But law, medicine, politics! The very idea was shocking. Very few women in the United States even had the right to vote in 1898. Jeannette decided to become a school teacher.

Socially, also, the university held little interest for her. She was an attractive young woman, of medium height, slender and graceful, with light brown hair, gray eyes and a friendly smile. She was a good dancer, but rarely attended the parties and dances at the university, preferring the company of her family.

On a sunny day in June, 1902, the Rankin clan proudly watched Jeannette receive her college diploma. No one attending the graduation exercises that day was prouder than John Rankin. That wonderful daughter of his! She would would do great things. He was sure of it. But he didn't live to see them. Two years later, he became ill and died. It was a great sorrow to his family, especially to Jeannette.

After graduation, Jeannette taught school, but soon discovered that she didn't enjoy teaching. She lived at home for the next few years, helping her mother run the house and wondering what to do with her life. Her sister Harriet was at college, the others in high school. Wellington was away at Harvard University, preparing to become a lawyer.

Jeannette missed Wellington and the discussions they used to have. Now she spent long evenings reading. In her search for knowledge, she came across a book by Jane Addams, the great lady who had founded Hull House, the famous social settlement in Chicago. Here was a woman who was trying to right some of the wrongs that Jeannette and Wellington used to talk about.

Jeannette was thrilled. She wrote a letter to her brother.

"Jane Addams' family is wealthy, and she could be leading a life of comfort and leisure. Instead she lives in a poor section of Chicago, among tenements and sweatshops, trying to help the people in the neighborhood.

"Old and young flock to Hull House. Boys and girls join reading and play-acting groups. Mothers who must work

leave their babies there to be fed and cared for.

"Miss Addams is also trying to get laws passed to do away with child labor, for a shorter working day and safe and sanitary working conditions for all workers. She has become known throughout the world as a leading social reformer."

As Jeannette Rankin read about Jane Addams and others who were devoting their lives to improving conditions in the United States, an idea began to grow within her. She, too, would devote her life to helping people.

A few months later, Jeannette, age 28, was on a train bound for New York City to prepare for a career in social work.

New York was a large, exciting city to Jeannette. She strolled along 5th Avenue, where elegant women came to buy the finest jewels and clothes in the world. She rode the trolley along Broadway, with its theaters and glittering marquees announcing plays and their star performers. She gazed up at the tall apartment houses along Riverside Drive, overlooking the calm waters of the Hudson River.

But in sections of the city that most visitors rarely saw, the conditions that Jane Addams had described now came alive for Jeannette Rankin. Here, for the first time in her life,

---

Jane Addams, the founder of Hull House in Chicago, and known throughout the world as a fighter for social reforms. Hull House became a model for other settlement houses. *(Sophia Smith Collection, Smith College)*

★ *21*

Jeannette, at about the time she left for New York City. (*Schlesinger Library, Radcliffe College*)

Jeannette saw poverty that made her shudder. It did not yet exist in the new West.

Many cities on the east coast had been built more than 100 years ago, before the American Revolution. The houses were old, without heat, with toilets in the hallway or the back yard. Large families of as many as ten lived crowded together in two or three small rooms. On the hard, treeless sidewalks Jeannette saw skinny, half-starved children playing in the dirty streets, and unemployed people walking listlessly, wondering where to find work.

In New York City, she also learned about the struggle going on for woman suffrage. As part of her education, Jeannette worked as an assistant to an experienced social worker. One day, the lady sent her out to get some pamphlets about woman suffrage. Most women in the United States did not have the right to vote in 1909. Missoula newspapers rarely wrote about the subject. When they did, it was generally to ridicule the women working in the suffrage movement.

Jeannette borrowed the pamphlets, took them to her room, and began to read. It was past midnight when she stopped, horrified at what she had learned.

The following weekend she went to visit Wellington at college. "Do you know that in faraway New Zealand women have been voting since 1893? And that here in our country, right now in 1908, four states—imagine!—only four states give women that right."

Wellington was as surprised as she was. "What states?" he asked.

★ 23

"Wyoming, Utah, Colorado and Idaho." She remembered them well. "We're one half of the population and we're not permitted to vote! Do you realize how unfair it is, how undemocratic?" she asked angrily.

"I do," Wellington said, recalling his sister's charges of "unfair" during their youthful late-into-the-night discussions. "What are you going to do about it?"

Jeannette had been too disturbed to think so far ahead. She knew that she would first have to finish her studies and get a job.

After graduating as a social worker, she found a position in an orphanage in Spokane, Washington. Here children who had no parents lived and were taken care of.

Jeannette looked forward to her job. She would be able to help children. But again she was disappointed. The children at the orphanage were treated badly, without love or affection. She tried to change things, but found that she couldn't.

Disillusioned, Jeannette left the orphanage. She was convinced that social workers could not solve the problems of the poor. There had to be other ways. She went to Seattle to study economics and sociology at the University of Washington, hoping to find solutions to slums, unemployment and homeless children.

It was 1910, a fortunate time for Jeannette Rankin to be in the state of Washington. The people were preparing for an election to vote on woman suffrage. This might be the answer, Jeannette thought. Women were more sensitive than men. If they were given the right to vote, they would elect good people who would pass good laws.

It didn't take long for Jeannette to get involved. She obtained posters saying "Vote for Women," and placed them on fences, lamp posts, store windows, wherever people would see them. The women in the suffrage movement heard about her. "We would like you to work with us, Miss Rankin," one of the leaders said. "You seem to be able to handle things well." Jeannette was delighted.

Her first job was to organize a meeting in Ballard, a small community on the outskirts of Seattle. For two days she distributed leaflets and contacted people who might be interested.

On the way to the meeting hall, she passed a group of children marching up and down the street waving flags. She stopped to ask what game they were playing. "Woman suffrage," they said, laughing. "It's funny." They had learned from their parents' conversation that suffrage for women was ridiculous.

Only eight people came to the meeting that day. Jeannette had not been told that Ballard was an anti-suffrage community.

But she did not give up. She continued to work with the suffrage women, learning about people, laws and elections. It was exciting. And when Election Day came and the women won, it was doubly exciting. She—Jeannette Rankin—had played a part in the victory.

Washington was now the fifth state in which women could vote. Forty-one more states to go. There was still much work to be done before all women in the nation would have the right to vote.

Jeannette had helped the women of Washington to victory. Could she lead a campaign for woman suffrage in her own state? She thought about it as she returned to her room after learning the results of the election.

Women and children march for suffrage.
(*Library of Congress*)

★ 27

3

A Fierce Battle

THE STRUGGLE FOR WOMAN SUFFRAGE HAD BEGUN IN 1869. THREE YEARS later, it was given great publicity by Susan B. Anthony, a former school teacher. The people—the men, that is—were preparing to vote for the president of the United States.

"I'm a citizen and I intend to vote," announced the brave Miss Anthony to her fellow-suffragettes.

She went to the polls and cast her ballot. For breaking the law, she was arrested, taken into court, tried and found guilty. The judge sentenced her to pay a fine of one hundred dollars. "I refuse to do so," she declared. "Resistance to tyrants is obedience to God." The American revolutionists had made the same protest to the King of England a hundred

Susan B. Anthony, pioneer for woman suffrage. The woman's suffrage amendment to the Constitution of the United States was called the Anthony Amendment in her honor. *(Sophia Smith Collection, Smith College)*

years before, regarding laws that they considered unjust.

The struggle for woman suffrage moved slowly.

In December of 1910, Jeannette Rankin returned home in time to spend Christmas with her family. She told them about her experiences in Washington. Wellington, who was now a lawyer and active in politics, informed her that a Montana lawmaker was planning to introduce a bill calling for a vote on woman suffrage.

Jeannette went to see the man. He laughed when she brought up the subject. "I was only joking," he said. "Do it anyhow," she urged. "I will," he agreed, "if you will come and tell the legislature why women should vote. Will you?"

Jeannette knew that this would not be an easy job. The lawmakers had considered the matter of woman suffrage a number of times before, and each time had turned it down. In addition, she had never before spoken before a large audience. "There's always a first time," she thought, then answered firmly, "I will."

With Wellington's help, she prepared a speech and rehearsed it over and over until she knew every word of it by heart. On the day set for the occasion, she entered the meeting hall beautifully dressed in a lace dress, a large-brimmed, stylish hat and a long string of pearls. Her eyes gleamed with excitement. In the history of Montana, no woman had ever before addressed the lawmakers. The hall and platform were decorated with flowers for the occasion.

Jeannette was a bit nervous as she was introduced. The room was crowded with people standing in the aisles and against the walls. Jeannette smiled and began to speak—about the early years, when Montana was still a rough, undeveloped territory. "The women of Montana worked side by side with their husbands to build this land into a fine state with homes, farms, lumber mills, factories and schools to educate our children. They are as capable as their husbands. I'm not saying more capable," she added with a twinkle in her eyes. The men and women in the audience laughed. "Now they should have the right to vote for laws to protect their homes, their children and themselves."

Jeannette spoke gently, but with conviction. Each time she made a point, she emphasized it by shaking her finger. There was great applause when she finished.

All of Montana heard of Jeannette Rankin. But it took several more years before she was able to win the vote for the women of her home state.

News of Jeannette spread to the leaders of the suffrage movement on the east coast. Harriet Laidlaw, head of the Woman Suffrage Party, offered her a job and a salary if she would come to New York to work for the party.

"I'm leaving in a week," she announced to her family. It was 1911. She packed her bags and went.

One of her duties was to hold street corner meetings. This was a strange and new experience for her. How could she attract an audience? She thought of a clever trick. She asked some friendly looking people to stop. As she talked with them, others gathered. Soon Jeannette had an audience.

One day she received a call from Mrs. Carrie Chapman Catt, head of the National American Suffrage Association. Mrs. Catt had become the leader of the suffrage movement after the death of Susan B. Anthony.

"I've been watching your work, Jeannette. You're an excellent organizer, a fine leader. How would you like to travel over the country for us?" "I would love it," Jeannette answered.

Soon she was being sent to Wisconsin, Ohio, Florida, Michigan—wherever the suffragettes needed help to organize a club or run an election. She spoke to legislators to persuade them to add a suffrage amendment to their state constitutions. She arranged for posters to be put up in halls where politicians were scheduled to speak. "Remember," she told the women, "it's the men who have to vote on the question of woman suffrage." It took many people and many months of hard work to prepare for an election.

But the struggle for woman suffrage was moving too slowly for its hard-working members. They needed publicity so that everyone in the nation would know about them.

Woodrow Wilson had been elected president of the United States, and would be taking office on March 4, 1913. Washington would be crowded with people to attend the ceremonies. That was the time to bring the cause of woman suffrage to the attention of the nation!

On March 3, with the city over-flowing with visitors, thousands of women from every state marched proudly down Pennsylvania Avenue. Jeannette led the delegation from Montana. An all-woman band played marching music and colorful banners waved in the air.

Men lined the streets on both sides. As the women marched by, they spit on them, tripped them up, called them names, threw lighted cigars at them. Most of the policemen were in sympathy with the men, and did little to protect the women. The situation became so dangerous that the army had to be called to restore order.

Just as the trouble had been unexpected, so were the headlines in all the newspapers of the country. The women had gotten the publicity they wanted!

Jeannette continued her work for the Suffrage Association until 1914. By then, the women in ten states had the privilege of voting. Although women in the western states were making more progress than those in the eastern states, Jeannette's home state was not among them. "It's time for the women of Montana," Jeannette wrote to her family. "I'm coming home." The Rankin family agreed unanimously.

Jeannette went into action. With the Montana suffragettes and several of her New York friends who came to help, they traveled to every part of the state, by automobiles and by horse-drawn carriages. Some even traveled on horseback. They spoke to the miners before the men entered the mines to begin the day's work, and to the miners' wives as they worked

★ *33*

in their kitchens. They visited farms and ranches. They shocked the citizens of Montana by speaking on street corners from open cars and wagons. They spoke in union halls and at

picnics. Jeannette even went into the schools to talk to the children about why their mothers ought to vote. "To protect you and your homes," she said. "Talk to your father. Remind

Suffragettes arriving in Washington, D.C.
(*Library of Congress*)

★ 35

him that we live in a democracy, and that your mother should have the same right to vote as he has." The children went home with bands around their hats inscribed with the words: Votes for Women.

Jeannette traveled thousands of miles and made hundreds of speeches. By now, she had the power to persuade people, and she always told the truth. The people liked this friendly woman and her direct manner of speaking.

Other people disagreed with Jeannette Rankin and with woman suffrage. The liquor interests—those people who made and sold liquor—were afraid that if women had the right to vote, they would pass laws prohibiting the sale of liquor, and that they, the liquor people, would be put out of business. The rich owners of the copper mines were afraid that women would cause them great expense. Women would demand that safety improvements be made in the mines for the protection of the miners, and workmen's compensation for workers who were injured in the frequent mine accidents.

Opposition came even from women. The wealthy ones who lived in great comfort could not understand the needs of less fortunate women. They joined with the liquor and copper people against the suffragettes.

If those weren't troubles enough, the bank in which the suffragettes had put their money went out of business. It was the money they needed so badly to pay the rent for meeting halls, printing, postage and other expenses. Nothing discouraged Jeannette and her faithful band of women. They started another fund-raising drive and went on working.

On Election Day, November 3, 1914, the men of Montana went to the polls and voted to give the women of their state the right to vote! Montana had become the 11th state in the union to add a suffrage amendment to its constitution.

Now Jeannette could rest—but only for a while. Another idea was dancing around in her mind—an exciting, challenging, daring idea.

Buttons for
woman suffrage.
(Library of Congress)

4

An Outrageous Idea

★ ▬▬ ★

"SUFFRAGE IS ONLY THE FIRST STEP TOWARD WOMEN'S EQUALITY, ladies, and most women in our country still do not enjoy this basic right. There is more, much more to be done. We must have women in government to help get it done."

Jeannette was addressing the women sitting in her parlor in Missoula. Two years before they had worked with her to bring suffrage to the women of Montana. They ranged in age from twenty to sixty, and in dress from elegant city fashions to simple country clothes. But they were united by one great passion—the freedom and welfare of women.

As Jeannette paused, the women nodded and murmured, "We must indeed have women in government. Women can govern as well as men. Of course we agree with you."

When the room was quiet, Jeannette continued in a low voice. "I want to run for the Congress of the United States." This was the first announcement of her plans. She had discussed the matter only with Wellington.

For a moment, there was dead silence, then a babel of voices, amazed and unbelieving.

"Why, Jeannette, there's never been a woman in Congress."

"You'll never be elected."

"Why don't you run for a lower office?"

"Yes. Start in the State Assembly. We'll work for you there."

For another hour, questions, answers, arguments filled the room. Jeannette tried to still their doubts. She closed with her most convincing argument.

"Ladies, there *must* be a woman in Congress. Only a woman will work for the right of all American women to vote. Only a woman will work for an amendment to the United States Constitution giving women that right. Just being there will make it harder for a man to vote *against* such an amendment."

The women knew Jeannette's ability. But much as they admired and respected her, they would not endorse a woman for one of the highest offices in the land. The idea was outrageous.

After the women left, Jeannette remained seated, her fingers braided together in her lap. She had hoped, she had

★ *39*

tried, but the women were not ready. They had not come as far as she had in their thinking. Without their help, could she convince the citizens of Montana to elect her to the Congress of the United States?

She was disturbed by another matter—a grave one. War had been waging in Europe for two years. It had started in 1914 between Great Britain and Germany. Soon, the three leading European powers—Britain, France and Russia—were fighting against Germany and Austria-Hungary. By 1916, most of the countries of the world had become involved.

Some Americans were urging that the United States send soldiers to help the British. President Wilson was opposed. He wanted to keep the country at peace. But in May, 1915, an event occurred that changed the course of American life. An English ship, the Lusitania, was sunk by a German submarine, and more than 100 American passengers were drowned. The pressure on the President to enter the war against Germany became great.

Deep in thought, Jeannette had not noticed that the sun had set and the room was getting dark. She rose from her chair, pushed back the soft brown hair from her face, and lit the lamps. Tomorrow morning she would go to see her brother, give him a report and hear what he had learned. Wellington had offered to find out what some of the political leaders thought about a woman in Congress. She dared to hope that he would have better news than she had.

Next day she sat in her brother's sunny, booklined office

Jeannette and her brother Wellington in front of the family home in Missoula, Montana. *(Montana Historical Society, Helena, Montana)*

in Helena, the capital of Montana, and told him about the meeting. "They were shocked at the idea. Called it outrageous." Her voice was gloomy.

Wellington's voice was just a little less gloomy. "So were the people I spoke with. Keep your sister from making a fool of herself," they advised.

Both were silent for a few moments. Jeannette broke the silence. "What do *you* think, Wellington?" She knew she would get an honest answer from her brother.

Wellington folded his arms on his large mahogany desk and leaned toward his sister. "You can do it, Jeannette. Your work for the suffrage movement made you the best known woman in Montana. You can get the nomination, and you can win the election." His voice was sure.

Jeannette was cheerful as she rose to leave. "Thanks, Wellington. Thanks." She kissed him on the cheek. "If I run, will you be my campaign manager?" she asked hesitantly. "You bet I will, and I'll get you elected," he promised. They both laughed as he walked with her to the door.

While driving home, Jeannette thought about Wellington's advice. He had not only urged her to run, he had offered to pay for her campaign. But without the help of those capable women. . . . For the next few months, she was busy talking to political leaders to learn how much support she could get.

In less than two years after Montana women had gained the right to vote, one of them was running for one of the highest offices in the country. Even more astonishing—for the first time in the history of the United States a woman was running for Congress.

As soon as Jeannette announced her candidacy, the women who had doubted her came to her support as they had done before. She would be running against three men. She was young, intelligent, attractive. Could she beat them?

The Rankin family came out in full force to work in her campaign. Wellington was her manager as he had promised. Harriet, Mary, Grace and Edna spoke to the voters. The women who had worked with her for woman suffrage did the same. As they had done two years before, they traveled all over the state. Montana was large, the roads rough, the mountains rugged.

Jeannette, about the time she was running for her first term in Congress. *(Sophia Smith Collection, Smith College)*

Jeannette spoke to the women: "I will work for child labor laws to protect your children and for education laws to educate them. I will work for an eight-hour work day for women and for the same rights to jobs and education as men have. And I will work for a suffrage amendment to the Constitution of our country so that *all* American women will have the right to vote."

To the workingmen she said: "I will work for safe and sanitary working conditions in mines, forests, factories, wherever people work."

And to the mothers and fathers of Montana who were frightened by the European war, she made a solemn promise: "I will do everything in my power to keep our country out of war and your sons safe at home."

Jeannette now had to fight against the same enemies she had fought before—the mine owners, the liquor interests, and the rich women who did not believe in rights for all women. They sent people out to talk against "that woman who wants to be in Congress." "A woman's place is in the house," said one speaker. Jeannette's answer was, "Yes, in the House of Representatives." "Politics is a dirty business," said another. "Women don't belong in it." Jeannette quickly retorted, "Who made it dirty?"

Jeannette's popularity grew. The people believed her. Her good sense and sincerity appealed to the working men and women of Montana. "She'll work for us down there in Washington," they told their neighbors.

On Election Day, Jeannette's friends called everyone who had a telephone. "Good morning. Have you voted for Jeannette Rankin?" they asked in a cheery voice.

In spite of her strong spirit, the next few days were difficult ones for Jeannette. There were no counting machines, and votes had to be counted by hand. Meanwhile reports had her losing, then winning, and with them went Jeannette's hopes.

At last, the final count came in. Headlines blazed the result in newspapers all over the world:

FIRST WOMAN ELECTED TO THE CONGRESS OF THE UNITED STATES!

5

A Lady in Congress

★ ▬▬▬ ★

AT 12 NOON ON APRIL 2, 1917, JEANNETTE RANKIN ENTERED THE GREAT hall of Congress. Dressed in a dark blue silk suit and carrying a large bouquet of flowers presented to her by the suffragettes that morning, all eyes were on her. Before she could reach her seat, her fellow-congressmen rushed up to congratulate her and shake hands. A few minutes later, the clerk of the House of Representatives began to call the roll. When he reached her name, everyone in the hall, both congressmen and visitors in the gallery, stood up and cheered. With a warm, radiant smile, the new congresswoman rose and bowed.

The early part of the day was a routine one. Jeannette and the other new members were formally admitted. The

On the way to her first session in Congress on April 2, 1917. Standing beside Jeannette is Mrs. Carrie Chapman Catt, national leader of the suffrage movement. *(Sophia Smith Collection, Smith College)*

Speaker, who acts as chairman of the House of Representatives, was elected, and preparations were made for the evening, when the urgent business of the day was to take place. President Wilson had called a special joint session of Congress to deliver an important speech.

At 8:30 in the evening of April 2, 1917, President Woodrow Wilson entered the House chamber. The hall was filled with members of both houses, and the gallery was jammed with visitors.

President Wilson had promised to keep the United States out of the war in Europe. But the sinking of the Lusitania had changed the feelings of many people. The President was now asking Congress for a formal declaration of war against Germany and her allies. "This is a war to make the world safe for democracy," he said, "a war to end all wars."

Congresswoman Rankin listened intently. She had guessed at the purpose for this extraordinary session. But to actually hear the call to war! She was suffering deeply. She knew that within a few days she would have to vote on the matter.

On April 4, the issue came before the Senate for a vote. Soon it would come before the House of Representatives. But before that, Jeannette was eager to hear the senators as they debated. Most of their arguments were in favor of a declaration of war. A few senators were opposed. Among these were Senator Robert LaFollette of Wisconsin and Senator George Norris of Nebraska, two men whom Jeannette knew and respected. The debate lasted four hours. Then the senators voted—82 for war, six against! Jeannette was horrified at the large number that voted for war.

The next day, Thursday, April 5, the House of Representatives met. The gallery was crowded with visitors, many particularly interested to hear how the new lady representative would vote on a matter of grave concern to every citizen in the nation.

The suffragettes were there. "The suffrage movement will suffer if you vote no," they said. Her brother was there. "You will not be reelected if you vote no," he warned. The pacificists were there. "Stay with your convictions," they urged. "We are with you."

Jeannette heard them all. She knew she would have to listen to her own conscience and make up her own mind. For her, war was a matter of life and death. She listened carefully to the debate among her fellow-representatives.

"We must help Britain defeat Germany."

"We have no right to interfere in a war in Europe."

"We cannot let our friends down."

"We must keep America out of foreign wars."

When Congressman Claude Kitchin of North Carolina arose, tears were streaming down his face. With a sob in his voice he said: "It takes neither moral nor physical courage to declare a war for others to fight." Congresswoman Rankin cried, too.

Jeannette knew that war weakened democracy, that people lost their rights of freedom of speech and of the press.

Already those people and newspapers who were in favor of staying out of the war were being called "unpatriotic."

Jeannette thought of the Montana parents to whom she had made the promise, "I will do everything in my power to keep our country out of war and your sons safe at home."

She thought of her brother's warning, "You will not be reelected if you vote no."

To be in Congress and help make laws for her country was important to Jeannette. But could she send young men to kill or be killed so that she could remain in Congress?

War was evil, her conscience told her. War was barbaric. The world was now civilized. There were other ways to solve conflicts between nations. They could talk things over, they could compromise differences. Chief Joseph and the Nez Perce Indians—they had found a way.

Jeannette felt that deep down in their hearts, the American people did not want war. They had never given the government the authority to plunge the nation into war. If the people themselves could vote on this matter that so deeply affected their lives, she was sure there would be no war. Jeannette didn't believe that this war would end all wars. Violence only led to more violence.

The debate raged all day and through the night.

On Friday morning, April 6, at 3 A.M., the roll was called. "Representative Rankin." All eyes fell on Jeannette. She didn't answer. There would be another call. She needed every minute she could get to consider, to listen to her conscience, to strengthen her courage. There had been some votes against the war, but not many. Did she have the courage to be one of the few? Words she had heard as a young girl came to her mind, "You do what is right because it is right, not because of the consequences."

The clerk was calling the names of those who hadn't answered before. "Miss Rankin."

Jeannette rose. Grasping the seat in front to keep herself steady, she said in a low clear voice, "I want to stand by my country, but I cannot vote for war. I vote no!" Forty-nine representatives voted with Jeannette Rankin against war, 373 representatives voted for war. Fifty representatives and six senators—these were hardly enough to keep the United States at peace.

Jeannette's troubles were not yet over. Newspapers called her a disgrace to womanhood, evidence that women were not yet capable of holding office. This accusation was the hardest blow of all.

Jeannette knew that her career in Congress was over. But her conscience was clear. She still had her term of two years ahead of her. There was much work for her to do.

Jeannette was now living in a large apartment in Washington, D.C. with her mother, her sister Harriet whose husband had died, and Harriet's two young children. Her

A reunion in Washington in 1937 of Jeannette Rankin and ten of the fifty-six senators and representatives who voted against America's entry into World War I. They are (seated left to right) Senator Ernest Lundeen, Representative Harold Knutson, former Representative Jeannette Rankin, Senator George Norris and former Representative Royal C. Johnson. Standing, left to right: Former Representatives Harry E. Hull, Edward Keating, C.C. Dill, Fred A. Britten, James A. Frear and Edward E. Browne.

mother took care of the apartment, and Harriet worked in Jeannette's office in the House Office Building where the representatives carried on their correspondence and received visitors. Jeannette had to have three secretaries to handle the great amount of mail, telephone calls and visitors who came to the office to discuss problems. Some just came to see what a lady lawmaker looked like. They were greeted by a young woman of 36, smiling and glowing with friendliness.

Jeannette got along well with the other members of Congress. A few, resenting this lone female among them, were merely courteous. Most were friendly and helpful. As a newcomer, she often had to turn to them for advice. It didn't take them long to recognize her fine mind. Then they, in turn, consulted her on legislative matters and developed great respect for her opinions. As they worked together, they found that few among them could match the enthusiasm, determination and thoroughness with which she approached the problems of a lawmaker. They appreciated the humor with which she lightened many serious moments.

Bills relating to the war were being passed in Congress. Though Jeannette had campaigned to keep America out of the war, now that the country was in it, she supported what had to be done. But she never forgot the promises she had made to the people back home in Montana.

The new congresswoman introduced a number of bills connected with the health, education and welfare of the men, women and children of the United States.

★ 53

Representative Rankin gives her first speech in Congress in 1917. *(National Archives)*

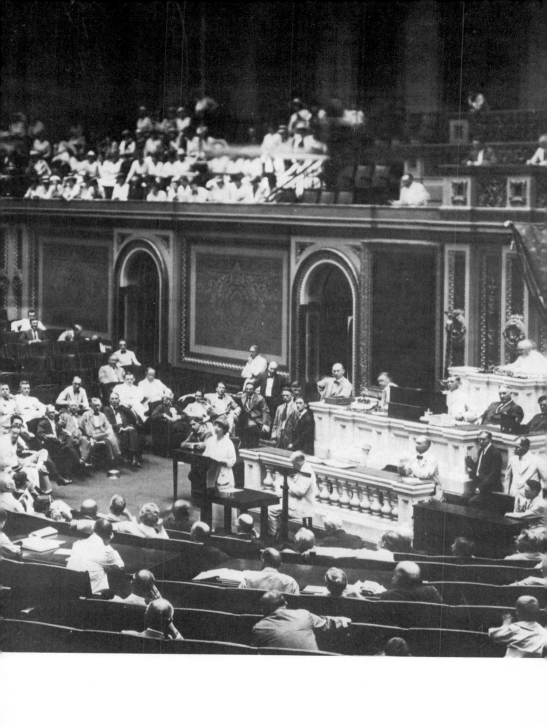

· There were few doctors in rural areas of the country, and many infants and mothers died. Representative Rankin introduced a bill to set up medical clinics for children, and for instructing mothers-to-be in health and hygiene and in how to take care of their new born babies. To those who opposed the bill, she retorted: "The government has always offered instruction in the hygiene of pigs, why not of people?"

She worked for the establishment of child care centers for young children while their mothers worked, and for safe and sanitary conditions for workers in factories, mills and mines.

She worked for a bill providing equal job opportunities and equal pay for women and men in war industries and in civil service. She forced the Bureau of Printing and Engraving, where money is printed, to improve conditions for the women who worked as long as fifteen hours a day, with little rest and no vacations.

She urged that laws be passed to abolish the employment of children in industry, declaring that child labor was cruel. She recommended better education for young people. "They will be our future leaders," she said.

She introduced a bill for the government to give financial help to poor families whose men were in the army or navy.

When news reached her that many men had been burned to death in a fire in a Montana mine, she was horrified. The company owners had not obeyed the safety laws, and the miners went out on strike. Jeannette asked the government to take control of the copper mines and operate them. "Our country needs copper for the war effort," she said, "and our miners need safe conditions in the mines so that their very lives are not in danger."

Some of the bills that Jeannette Rankin introduced were passed while she was in Congress. Others were passed at a later time.

Jeannette continued to press for an amendment to the Constitution that would give all American women the right to vote. It was called the Anthony Amendment, in honor of Susan B. Anthony, the famous pioneer in woman suffrage. But President Wilson was not sympathetic to the cause.

The suffragettes went to work, Jeannette inside Congress, the others outside. With the help of Alice Paul, a brilliant young woman who had been jailed in England for working for woman suffrage, they set up a picket line in front of the White House. In rain and shine, well-dressed women marched back and forth. Bus loads of women came from all parts of the country to help. When one group tired, another took its place. The women carried signs and banners saying: "Democracy should begin at home, Mr. President." "How long must women wait for liberty?" Many were arrested and taken to a jail filled with rats and vermin, where they were beaten and tortured. They went on a hunger strike to protest their treatment. Some almost died.

Jeannette visited the jail, and could hardly believe what she saw. When she threatened to call for an investigation, the prison officials were afraid of the publicity, and the women were quickly released.

A suffrage amendment had first been introduced in Congress in 1878, and in every Congress thereafter. Forty years later, congressmen still disagreed on the subject. However, the President had finally become convinced of a woman's right to vote.

In January of 1918, Representative Rankin brought the Anthony Amendment up for a vote in the House of Representatives. She was granted the privilege of opening the discussion. Using her most powerful arguments, Jeannette reminded the members that women had helped in the war effort, doing the same hard and dangerous work as men, making bombs, building ships, melting steel. She spoke of democracy. "The United States fought the war to make the world safe for democracy. Surely the gentlemen present are aware that women are part of the world," she said wryly. "Surely you realize that women are also capable of doing the world's work."

Feelings ran high, and the debate was heated. When the members were finally ready to vote, four congressmen who had promised to support Jeannette came from sickbeds to keep their promises. One had to be carried on a stretcher.

The voting was a time of tension for the lone congress-woman and the suffragettes crowding the gallery. The clerk took the first roll call. The vote was close, too close for comfort. He called the role a second time.

Passed! The Anthony Amendment had passed! By one vote, but passed! The women sighed with relief, then shouted with joy. They came rushing down to hug and kiss their wonderful friend in Congress. There were tears, too, tears of happiness after the long years of hard work. Jeannette's tears mingled with those of all the others.

The bill now went before the Senate, where it lost by two votes. But the following year, in 1919, the senators again voted and passed it. The following year, when Jeannette was no longer in Congress, it was approved by the states and became the 19th amendment to the Constitution of the United States. After more than 50 years of work by thousands of women, millions of American women went proudly to the polls in the 1921 election.

The Anthony Amendment was written simply and clearly—the women had seen to that—so that there could be only one interpretation. It states:

"The right of citizens of the United States to vote shall not be denied or abridged by the United States or by any State on account of sex.

"Congress shall have the power to enforce this article by appropriate legislation."

In 1919, Jeannette's term in Congress was over. "I will be back some day," she told her friends.

"What are you going to do now?" they asked.

For a woman concerned with the welfare of her country and the problems of the world, there was much to do. She wondered where to begin. An unexpected letter helped her make a decision.

6

A Lobbyist
for Peace

EDUCATION AND PROTECTION OF CHILDREN. SAFE WORKING
conditions for working people. A shorter work week. And
peace! Without peace, no improvements in living would be
of much value.

All of these thoughts ran through Jeannette's mind as
she cleared her desk in preparation for leaving Washington.
Her office was no longer the busy place it had been when
she first came there. She picked up the morning mail and
quickly looked through it, selecting one letter from all the
rest. It was from New York. She opened it and read quickly.

"Look at this, Harriet." She showed the letter to her
sister. "Dear Representative Rankin: You have been named as

a delegate to the Women's International Conference for Permanent Peace." The conference was to be held in Zurich, Switzerland, at the same time that men representing the countries that had been at war were meeting in Versailles, a suburb of Paris, to draw up a peace treaty. The women, representing a number of countries, were coming together to discuss the treaty and make suggestions to the treaty-makers that would guarantee peace to the world.

"That's marvelous, Jeannette, just marvelous!" Harriet was enthusiastic. "You may be able to help this crazy world out of it's muddle."

Jeannette laughed. "I'll try, Harriet. You can be sure I'll try."

In May 1919, Jeannette left for Switzerland with six other American delegates. Among them were Jane Addams, the lady who had established the famous settlement house in Chicago, and whose work had greatly influenced Jeannette's life.

In Zurich, the American women met with delegates from other countries who had fought in the war as allies or as enemies. The women of both sides wanted peace for their children and grandchildren, and all the other children in the world. They drew up a list of recommendations and sent them to President Wilson who was at Versailles. His answer came quickly. He was in complete sympathy with the ladies, he said, but he could not convince the men to make any changes in the treaty that they had drawn.

The women knew from newspaper reports that the treaty

was a harsh one; that it made great demands on the defeated countries. Such a treaty, they felt would only produce anger and hatred and more wars. They were greatly disappointed that their recommendations had not been considered.

A woman from Austria spoke. "We women must begin to work for a permanent peace so that our families and our nations will never go to war again. We cannot leave this matter to men." A cheer went up. Meeting face to face had created a strong feeling of friendship between the women. They set to work. Before the conference was over, they had organized the Women's International League for Peace and Freedom to abolish war forever. The League still exists today. In 1973, it helped to bring an end to the Vietnam War.

On the way home, Jeannette and some of her friends visited London and attended a session of the House of Commons. They saw the ladies' gallery, which the Englishwomen called "the monkey cage." Here the women who had struggled for suffrage had chained themselves to the bars and shouted their demands to the members of Parliament.

Back in the United States, Jeannette returned to Washington and to the causes to which she had dedicated her life—people and peace. She got a job with an organization concerned with the welfare of working people. She would be a lobbyist for them—a person who speaks to lawmakers to persuade them of her cause.

She talked to many congressmen, trying to convince them to pass laws for better working conditions. She was

★ 63

particularly concerned about children, and urged the congressmen to prohibit their employment in the United States. She had presented many of these laws during her term in Congress.

Changes were made—but slowly—over a period years. It wasn't until the 1930s that an eight-hour day was introduced into industry. The five-day work week began in the 1940s.

In 1938, the Fair Labor Standards Act was passed. It provided that only boys and girls sixteen years of age and over may be employed in industry, except in dangerous jobs. The minimum age for dangerous jobs, such as mining, was set at eighteen.

After several years of lobbying for labor laws, Jeannette became a lobbyist for peace. For the next ten years, she lobbied for the National Council for the Prevention of War. Her chief concern was for a constitutional amendment to outlaw war.

"We must make war illegal, unconstitutional," she pleaded with the lawmakers in Washington. She reminded them of the thousands of young men who had died or been wounded in World War I. "We must not let this happen again."

She also lobbied for United States' membership in the World Court, which had been established in 1920 as the Permanent Court of International Justice. It was the first court in history to which the nations of the world could come to settle their disputes in a courtroom rather than on a battlefield.

Fifty-one nations joined the court, but Jeannette could not convince the Congress to do the same. Nor could she convince them of the importance of a constitutional amendment to make war a crime.

There were now several women in Congress. They seemed to be as war-minded as most of the men.

"I don't understand, Harriet," Jeannette complained with bitterness to her sister. "If men don't care about the human race, then women must. Surely they know that most people gain nothing from war."

Harriet sighed. "I know," she said sadly. "I know."

During summers and holidays, Jeannette returned to Montana and stayed at her brother's large ranch. Wellington had been married and divorced. Jeannette sometimes thought of marriage. But her work was more important to her.

During her travels through the country, she had taken a fancy to the state of Georgia. It would be a good place to live, she thought. There was the University of Georgia where she was sure to find people with similar interests to her own. It would be a good place to work for peace. And Washington, D.C. was not too far away.

In 1924, she bought sixty acres of land in Bogart, ten miles west of Athens, where the University of Georgia was located. Within a few days she built a low white house among the pines, her favorite trees. The house had one long room, a sleeping porch, and a red chimney, but no electricity. Jeannette cooked over a kerosene stove in a shed behind the house, and washed dishes near a well under a pine. All around the

★ 65

Finishing the house on her pecan farm in Georgia, which was built for her in four days. *(Sophia Smith Collection, Smith College)*

house she planted trees—hundreds of peach and pecan trees. At night, she listened to the mockingbirds sing under a brilliant moon. She never locked her doors.

Jeannette loved visitors, and invited her family and friends to come and enjoy the loveliness and simplicity of her rustic home. They came, and slept under the trees until she could add several more rooms to the house.

Jeannette became friendly with the families who lived on the neighboring farms. She talked to them about canning and pickling and peace. She believed that children should learn about peace when they were young, and organized them into two clubs. The girls came to her house on Saturday afternoons. They learned to bake graham bread and went swimming in a nearby pond. She told them stories about Jane Addams and the other women who had attended the peace conference in Switzerland. The boys came at night. A few played home-made instruments and the others danced. Jeannette spoke to them of Mahatma Gandhi, the courageous pacifist leader of India, and other great workers for peace.

With some students and professors at the University of Georgia, Jeannette organized a Georgia Peace Society. They worked together in a campaign against compulsory military training in high schools and colleges. "We cannot settle disputes by killing nice young men," she said in her speeches to the students. "We cannot get peace by spending millions of dollars for armaments. It is your world." She pointed her

As she had done years earlier, Jeannette addressed a peace rally—this time against the Vietnam War—at the University of Georgia in 1970. She was still popular with the students who often invited her to speak at their meetings. *(Schlesinger Library, Radcliffe College)*

finger at her audience. "You, the young people, must work for better understanding among nations to make this a safe world for yourselves and for future generations."

She urged them to write to their representatives in Congress. "Tell them to spend our taxes on homes, hospitals, schools. If enough people write, they will listen, for it is the people who elect them. And they will answer you, too."

She followed her own advice, writing hundreds of letters. One day, she received an answer from a congressman who obviously believed that a woman's place was in the kitchen. It was a list of cookbooks. Jeannette laughed.

Many people of Georgia became her supporters. But those Georgians who didn't agree with her were disturbed to see the peace movement grow in their state. One of these was a newspaper publisher who accused her of being unpatriotic. Jeannette sued him and won her case.

The 1930s arrived, and with them an economic depression in the United States. Businesses were closing down. People were being fired from factories, stores, offices. Many wandered over the land in search of jobs, but there were none. By 1933, there were about fourteen million men and women out of work.

The rest of the world, too, was suffering an economic depression.

The German people had become poor and desperate by 1933. Their money was worthless because of wild inflation— it cost almost two billion marks to buy even a newspaper! Six million workers, or about half of the normal work force in Germany, were unemployed. They were ready to listen to anyone who would promise some help—any help. And they were willing to blame their miseries on anyone.

In that same year of 1933, Adolf Hitler, leader of the Nazi Party, became dictator of Germany. To take the peoples' minds off their troubles, Hitler began to preach hatred.

Hitler and the Nazis believed that the Germans were the purest descendants from the Aryans, an ancient race. Hitler said that Aryans were superior to all other people. "We must rid our country of the others."

He attacked all political parties that did not agree with the Nazis, and everyone else who did not agree with his ideas —scientists, writers, artists, engineers, teachers and others. He told lies about the Catholics, Gypsies, and Jews. He hated the Catholics because they disapproved of his campaign against religion and democracy. To him, the Gypsies were an inferior group who wandered over the land. However, he saved his most cruel attacks for the Jewish people.

Hitler blamed all the country's troubles on them, although they were citizens of Germany and had made valuable contributions to their country. Many Jews had become musicians, scientists, businessmen, philosophers and writers. Some had become world famous. But Hitler never forgot that as a young man he had applied for admission to an art school and was turned away, while Jewish students were being accepted. After one of his speeches, Hitler and his Nazi helpers gave hatchets to the members of the Nazi Party and told them to kill Jews.

In 1934, Hitler began to build up a huge army and navy. This was contrary to the Versailles Treaty which ended World War I. That treaty had forbidden Germany to increase its military forces or to build weapons of war.

Jeannette saw through Hitler's lies, though many people didn't. She knew that neither Jews, Gypsies nor Catholics threatened Germany—it was Hitler who threatened Germany, as well as the whole world. And yet the United States and Britain were selling armaments to Germany and lending the country money.

Jeannette was so worried that she went to Washington and spoke to as many congressmen as she could. "Hitler is a dangerous man, and a threat to world peace. We must stop giving him aid." She went to Europe, to the League of Nations at Geneva, Switzerland. "Hitler must be curbed," she warned, "or he will destroy the whole world." No one listened.

In the midst of her work and worries, Jeannette's home burned down. She bought another one several miles away, in Watkinsville, for $300. Its plumbing consisted of one faucet in the bathroom, but the house was surrounded by flowers and 49 acres of wild forest.

A friend gave her a dachshund called Sam. On sunny days, Jeannette and Sam walked through the woods. On cold nights, as she sat reading near her fireplace, he lay stretched out at her feet.

In the early 1930s, Jeannette Rankin prepares to leave Washington on a speaking tour calling for a peace plank in the Republican and Democratic party platforms. (*Wide World Photos*)

Jeannette now had a new outlet for her peace talks—the radio. On her first talk the microphone frightened her. She had always been able to look at her audience. But she quickly overcame her fear when she realized that she could reach more people by radio than she could in a union hall or at a picnic. She could bring her peace message to thousands of people, even millions in just one talk. It was exciting to think about. She made hundreds of radio speeches.

By 1938, Jeannette's fears for the world became real. In October, Britain and France agreed to Hitler's conquest of Czechoslovakia. Austria had been overrun in March. By the middle of 1939, Britain and France had begun to see that they made a terrible mistake by giving in to Hitler, when he had promised not to invade any more countries. And they knew that Poland would be next. So Britain and France told the Poles, and the world, that any invasion of Poland by Germany would mean war. They were not going to give up any more territory to Hitler.

Then on September 1, the German army invaded Poland. Bombs were dropped over cities, schools, shops and churches, over defenseless men, women and children. Two days later, Britain and France declared war against Germany. World War II had started.

Jeannette heard the news with horror. Would the United States stay out of this war? Or would they enter it as they did in World War I?

An old idea was beginning to gnaw at Jeannette. Almost a quarter of a century had passed since she first ran for Congress in 1916. Perhaps it was time to run again. Could she win after so many years away from Montana and her supporters? Many of them were no longer living. The new voters didn't know her. Most hadn't even been born when she first campaigned for Congress.

Jeannette was close to sixty and in good health. Nothing about her had changed, except her hair; it was now white. She was determined to try again.

7
One Woman
Against 388 Men

IT WAS NOW THE SPRING OF 1940. JEANNETTE WAS DISCUSSING HER
campaign with her brother.

"I'm going to start with the young people," she told
Wellington. "I must make them understand that there is no
glory in war. They must learn to regard war as they do canni-
balism. Today nobody in his right mind would eat another
person."

Jeannette visited the high schools and addressed the
students at their assemblies. She spoke of the war in Europe,
which was spreading over the world. The three leading European countries—Britain, France and the Soviet Union—were
fighting against Italy, Japan and Germany.

"War leads to more war," she informed her young

audience. "We must help other nations settle their disputes in a peaceful manner. But we must stay out of their wars."

She closed with the same advice she had given the students in Georgia. "You have a voice in your government. Use it. Write to your congressman. Write to your president. Tell your parents to write, too."

As she had done before, Jeannette visited the people in the cities and the countryside, in their kitchens and their shops. "If I am again elected to Congress, I will work to keep our country at peace and your sons at home."

The parents of young men who would be called to fight were afraid of another war. They believed Jeannette Rankin. They knew that she kept her word. When Election Day came, Jeannette was elected again. In March of 1941, she was back in Congress.

France had already fallen to the Nazis, and the German army continued its invasion of the other European countries. The Nazis seemed unstoppable. Only Britain and the Soviet Union were left to face them and their allies. The world was frightened.

The American government was sending huge amounts of food, ammunition and other supplies to Britain and the Soviet Union. The country was drawing closer and closer to war.

"Let us continue to help our friends, but let us stay out of their wars," Jeannette urged. "Foreign wars are no part of the American way of life."

She proposed that an election be held to learn what was

During her second term in Congress, Jeannette was no longer the only woman member. Here she is in 1941 with four other congresswomen (from left to right): Frances P. Bolton of Ohio, Mary T. Norton of New Jersey, Margaret Chase Smith of Maine, Edith Nourse Rogers of Massachusetts. *(United Press International Photo)*

the will of the people before declaring war. She had faith in the men and women of America. Some congressmen agreed with her. Most of them did not. Jeannette was desperate. She proposed other measures to keep the United States out of the war. They were all defeated.

On Sunday afternoon, December 7, 1941, people who were listening to their radios were suddenly shocked to hear: "Our program is being interrupted to bring you a special announcement. Japan has attacked Pearl Harbor. We repeat, Japan has attacked Pearl Harbor!" It was a surprise attack.

In the Far East, Japan had been taking territory from China which was America's friend. This friendship angered the Japanese because it interfered with their plans to conquer all of the Far East.

Things moved quickly in Washington. The following day, a resolution declaring war against Japan came before the House of Representatives for a vote. This time the debate lasted only forty minutes. Jeannette was determined to voice her opposition.

"Mr. Speaker, I wish to speak."

"You're out of order," snapped Speaker of the House, Sam Rayburn.

"Mr. Speaker, I wish to be heard." Again and again Jeannette rose and tried to speak, but without success. Shouts of "Sit down! Sit down!" followed each attempt.

The roll was called. The votes came quickly. "Aye." "Aye." "Aye." Not a single "nay," so far. It had been all

"Ayes" in the Senate, too. Had everyone gone crazy? Jeannette thought. Her name would soon be reached.

"Representative Rankin." Jeannette rose, and without a moment of hesitation answered firmly, "I vote no. As a woman I cannot go to war, and I refuse to send anyone else."

Angry shouts came from all parts of the hall. One nay against 388 ayes!

Jeannette knew that her vote would not change things. It was simply a protest vote against the horror of war. But she had to vote as her conscience told her. She knew no other way. It took courage to stand alone.

Some years later, John F. Kennedy, who was later to become president of the United States, called her one of the most fearless women in American history.

When Jeannette left the congressional chambers, the crowd outside was so angry at her that it looked like a riot. She had to hide in a telephone booth for safety, and was grateful when the police escorted her to her office. She locked the door, sank into a chair and put her hands over her face. Tears came streaming from her eyes. Was there no hope for mankind? Would people continue to destroy each other?

A few days later, Congress formally declared war against Germany as in World War I. The United States was again allied with Britain, France, and the Soviet Union against Germany, Italy and Japan. Soon most of the world was involved on one side or the other. It was another world war—World War II.

Escaping from an angry crowd into a telephone booth after her lone vote against the United States' entrance into World War II. *(United Press International Photo)*

New reports of German atrocities were coming in from Europe. Hitler was still persecuting the Jewish people, depriving them of rights and property, and putting them into concentration camps only because they were Jewish. He finally decided to kill all Jews in Germany and the conquered countries, and started on his plan for genocide—the extermination of a whole people. Those Jews who could escape fled to other lands. But most of them couldn't. Before the European war was over, almost 6,000,000 Jewish men, women and children had been put to death.

Aside from Jews, the Germans also killed millions of other innocent people. In the German occupied areas of the Soviet Union more than 30 million people were killed or died of hunger.

In every country they conquered, the Nazis had destroyed all political parties that opposed them. They were imprisoning artists, writers, scientists, and all others who disagreed with them. They were even burning books that they didn't like. Jeannette felt that these horrors would not have occurred if no help had been given to Germany in the early years of Hitler's rise.

Again Congress was busy with the war and gave little attention to bills for social improvement.

In 1943, when her term in Congress was over, Jeannette returned to the quiet woods and mountains of Montana, and her devoted and loving family. She lived at Wellington's ranch, and helped care for her mother, who was old and ill.

★ *81*

In Montana, riding Whitetail, her sister Edna's horse. (*Schlesinger Library, Radcliffe College*)

She visited with her sisters, and with her nieces and nephews.

All the Rankins had married except Jeannette, and all had children, except Wellington. In addition to his successful law practice, he was a leading figure in the political affairs of Montana. He had been an attorney general, a justice of the state supreme court, and had held several other important positions.

Jeannette's sisters had all pursued careers except one. Harriet had been dean of women at Montana State University. Mary had taught English at the university before getting married and raising a family. Edna, the first woman in Montana to study law, was deeply involved in the cause of family planning. Only Grace had not followed a career.

Although Jeannette was not active in politics, she kept herself informed of events in the country and the world.

Germany had been defeated, but the United States was still at war with Japan. To force a quick surrender, President Truman had ordered atomic bombs dropped on two Japanese cities, Hiroshima and Nagasaki. The atomic bomb was a new and deadly weapon which no one had ever experienced before.

Both cities were almost completely destroyed by just one bomb each. Hundreds of thousands of people died instantly. And thousands of others became ill, crippled or disfigured from radiation sickness.

A few days after the bombings, on August 14, 1945, Japan surrendered. The war was over, but the world was frightened. The new bomb was a horrible killer.

Jeannette's hatred of war had reached its highest point. She was miserable and there was nothing she could do. She became restless.

For a number of years she had been reading about Mahatma Gandhi, the Asian crusader for peace and the freedom of his country, India, a colony of the British Empire. Gandhi was known all over the world for his great courage and his love of peace. This thin, frail-looking man was leading a revolt and independence movement in India against the powerful British Empire. His belief that "in a gentle way you can shake the world" appealed to the gentle spirit of Jeannette Rankin. She was so stirred by what Gandhi was trying to accomplish that in 1946, at the age of 66, she boarded a ship for India.

8
Travel, Work and More Work

★ ▬▬▬ ★

UNDER THE LEADERSHIP OF MAHATMA GANDHI, THE PEOPLE OF INDIA were struggling to become a free and independent country, just as the American colonies had done about 200 years before. But Gandhi's methods were different.

This wise and holy man did not believe in violence. Using peaceful ways to attain his goal, he led his people on huge freedom marches. He urged them not to buy British-made goods. He went on hunger strikes to remind them to protest peacefully. And he often was sent to jail for breaking British laws against unlawful marching and meetings. His method was called "civil disobedience"—when laws are unjust, it is the duty of citizens to disobey them. In 1947, after

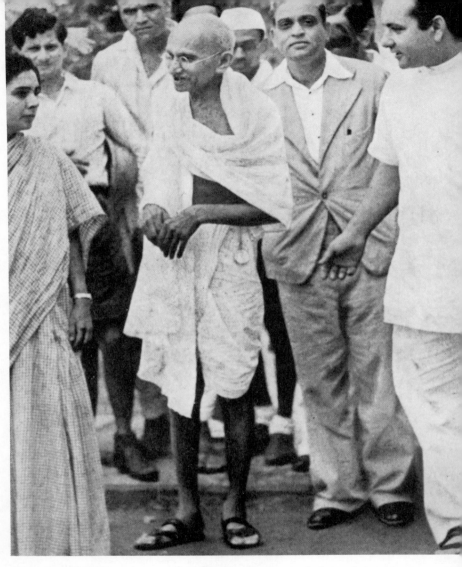

Mahatma Gandhi, in center, wearing glasses and dressed in a *lungi.*
(Library of Congress)

a quarter of a century of struggle, India became an independent nation.

Jeannette had brought her car with her on the ship. Now she drove through the cities and villages of India. She stopped to speak with people in the streets and children in the villages and the countryside. She saw slums, poverty and disease worse than she had seen in the United States.

For the next twenty years, Jeannette traveled to many countries. Everywhere she saw similar conditions. She was convinced that if nations spent less money for armaments, they would have more for homes, schools and hospitals.

In the mid 1960s, Jeannette returned home to find that American soldiers were being sent to Vietnam to fight a war going on in that distant land. "This is a war between the people of Vietnam," she exclaimed. "We have no right to interfere." When Women Strike for Peace, an anti-war group, asked her to lead a protest march to Washington, she readily agreed.

On a slushy, snowy day in January 1968, 87-year-old Jeannette Rankin, her cheeks rosy in the frosty air, led thousands of women to the Capitol. There Jeannette, Mrs. Martin Luther King and several more women went to the office of one of the leaders of Congress, and presented to him a petition to end the war and bring American soldiers home.

Members of women's liberation groups (once known as women's rights) learned about the oldest living suffrage

The Jeannette Rankin Peace
Brigade marching to the Capitol
in January, 1968 to protest the
Vietnam War. Thousands of
women came from all parts of the
country. Jeannette Rankin, wearing glasses, is in the center.
(United Press International Photo)

★ 89

leader, and invited her to speak at a meeting. "Run for Congress. Run for the Senate," she told them. "Make a better world for your children. Don't let the men run your lives."

In 1972, Jeannette Rankin, now 92 years old, flew to Washington D.C. where the National Organization of Women awarded her the Susan B. Anthony award as the living woman who had made the greatest contribution to women's rights.

Jeannette was now living in Carmel, California. Her brother Wellington had died some years before. But before he died, he had bought for her a modern studio apartment in a retirement home. Jeannette could not think of herself as retired. Although it was difficult for her to get around physically, her mind was still active. She still kept informed of the news, and wrote letters to the president about ways to attain a peaceful world.

On May 18, 1973, just a month before her 93rd birthday, she died peacefully in her sleep.

During one of her last speeches, a student asked what young people could do for their country. Her answer was, "Go on from where I leave off."

Receiving the first Susan B. Anthony award on February 12, 1972 from the National Organization of Women (NOW), for her great contributions to women's rights and as the outstanding living feminist. *(Sophia Smith Collection, Smith College)*

Index

Gypsies, 70, 71

H
Harvard University, 19
Helena, MT, 42
Hiroshima, atomic bomb
    dropped on, 83
Hitler, Adolf, 70, 71, 73, 81
House of Commons, England,
    63
House of Representatives, 44,
    46, 48, 49, 58, 78
Hudson River, 21
Hull House, 19
hunger strikes, 85

I
Idaho, 14, 24
Indians, 14, 15
Italy, 75, 79

J
Japan, 75, 78, 79, 83
Jews, 70, 71, 81

K
Kennedy, John F., 79
King of England, 28
King, Mrs. Martin Luther, 87
Kitchin, Congressman Claude,
    49

L
LaFollette, Senator Robert, 48
Laidlaw, Harriet, 31

League of Nations, 71
London, 63
Lusitania, 40, 48

M
medical clinics, 56
Michigan, 32
Missoula, MT, 13, 14, 15, 16,
    17, 23, 38
"monkey cage," 63
Montana, 13, 14, 15, 17, 30,
    31, 33, 34, 37, 38, 40, 43,
    44, 50, 53, 65, 74, 81
Montana State University, 83

N
Nagasaki, atomic bomb
    dropped on, 83
National American Suffrage
    Association, 32, 33
National Council for the
    Prevention of War, 64
National Organization of
    Women, 90
Nazi Party, 70, 71, 76, 81
Nebraska, 48
New Hampshire, 31
New York City, 21, 23, 31, 61
New Zealand, 23
Nez Perce Indians, 14, 15, 50
Norris, Senator George, 48

O
Ohio, 32
Oregon, 14

★ *93*

Rankin, Mary (sister), 13, 43, 83
Rankin, Olive Pickering, (mother), 12, 13, 17
Rankin, Philena (sister), 13
Rankin, Wellington (brother), 13, 16, 17, 19, 23, 24, 30, 39, 40, 42, 43, 65, 75, 81, 83, 90
Rayburn, Sam (Speaker of the House), 78
Russia, 40

S
Sam (dachshund), 71
Seattle, WA, 24, 25
Senate, United States, 48, 59, 79, 90
Soviet Union, 75, 76, 79, 81
Spokane, WA, 24
State Assembly, 39
suffrage movement. *See* woman suffrage
suffragettes, 32, 33, 36, 46, 49, 57, 58

T
Truman, President, 83

U
United States, 13, 17, 18, 21, 23, 28, 32, 34, 43, 48, 58, 59, 63, 69, 71, 73, 79, 83
University of Georgia, 65, 67

University of Montana, 17
University of Washington, 24
Utah, 24

V
Versailles, 62, 71
Vietnam War, 63, 87

W
Washington, D.C., 32, 51, 61, 63, 65, 71, 78, 87
Washington, state of, 24, 26, 27, 30
White House, 57
Wilson, President Woodrow, 32, 40, 48, 57, 62
Wisconsin, 32
Women's International Conference for Permanent Peace, 62
Women's International League for Peace and Freedom, 63
woman suffrage, 23, 25, 27, 28, 30, 32, 36, 43, 57
Woman Suffrage Party, 31
Women Strike for Peace, 87
World Court, 64
World War I, 64, 71, 73, 79
World War II, 73, 79
Wyoming, 24

Z
Zurich, Switzerland, 62, 67